M000229155

ESSENTIALS OF
HOLINESS

DAVID K. BERNARD

Essentials of Holiness

by David K. Bernard

©1989, David K. Bernard
  Reprint History: 1994, 1995, 1996, 1998, 2000, 2002
  Cover Design by Tim Agnew

All Scripture quotations in this book are from the King James Version of the Bible unless otherwise identified.

Printed in United States of America.

WORD AFLAME®PRESS
8855 DUNN ROAD
HAZELWOOD, MO 63042-2299

Library of Congress Catalogining-in-Publication Data

Bernard, David K., 1956
    Essentials of holiness / David K. Bernard.
        p. cm.
    Includes bibliographical references.
    ISBN 0-932581-55-2
    1. Holiness. 2. Oneness Pentecostal churches—Doctrines.
3. Pentecostal churches—Doctrines. I. Title.
BT767.B45 1989
234'.8—dc20   89-37905
                                                              CIP

To
Daniel
with
love

Contents

Preface

The purpose of this booklet is to present an overview of the doctrine and practice of biblical holiness. A number of ministers have expressed an interest in a small, inexpensive booklet on the subject to give to church members and new converts, and this booklet is offered to help meet that need. It has been written as (1) a resource tool and study aid for leaders, (2) a concise reference and refresher for believers, and (3) an introduction for new converts and interested inquirers.

The booklet grew out of a paper presented at the first biennial Symposium on Oneness Pentecostalism, which was held in St. Louis, Missouri, on January 8-10, 1986. The paper, entitled "The Theology of Holiness," was published in *Symposium on Oneness Pentecostalism 1986* (Hazelwood, MO: United Pentecostal Church International, 1986).

This work is not offered as denominational dogma, as a legalistic rulebook, or in a spirit of condemnation. It is simply an attempt to explore and enunciate basic Bible principles and apply them consistently. There may be differences of opinions on certain points, and it is not possible to discuss every topic thoroughly. Nevertheless, it is hoped that the reader will approach this material with an open mind and heart, consider it prayerfully, and study the relevant biblical passages. The conclusions expressed are valid only insofar as the Scriptures support them.

For a detailed discussion of the topics covered, see *In Search of Holiness* by Loretta Bernard and David Bernard, *Practical Holiness: A Second Look* by David Bernard, and *Holiness Seminar* (taped lectures) by David Bernard. Other booklets in the author's Essentials series are *Essentials Doctrines of the Bible, Essentials of Oneness Theology,* and *Essentials of the New Birth.*

ESSENTIALS OF HOLINESS

Introduction

Holiness is an old-fashioned, irrelevant concept to most people today, even in Christendom. Yet God has always commanded His people to be holy; holiness is essential to biblical Christianity. True Christians have traditionally emphasized holiness, rejecting as unholy various aspects of worldly lifestyle. In recent years, however, many professing Christian groups have discarded much of this teaching.

In studying and developing biblical holiness it is important to address several key questions. What is holiness? What are important principles of holiness, and how are we to apply them practically in our lives? How can we be holy, and why should we? Where do standards of holiness come from? Are they biblical or man-made? Are they universal and unchanging or cultural and temporary? How can we maintain scriptural holiness while avoiding legalism and upholding Christian liberty?

1. The Call to Holiness

The Bible calls followers of Christ to a life of holiness, and it stresses the essentiality of holiness. "Follow peace with all men, and holiness, without which no man shall see the Lord" (Hebrews 12:14).

The new birth is the initial experience of salvation, but

the work of salvation does not end there. There is also the continuing work of sanctification, a process of becoming progressively more Christ-like that begins at the new birth and leads to sinless perfection in the life to come. This work takes place as we submit daily to the leadership and control of the Holy Spirit (II Thessalonians 2:13).

Just as we must be born again to see the kingdom of God (John 3:3-5), so we must pursue holiness, or sanctification, in order to see the Lord. "Pursue peace with all men, and holiness, without which no one will see the Lord" (Hebrews 12:14, NKJV). "Make every effort to live in peace with all men and to be holy; without holiness no one will see the Lord" (NIV). The new birth will have no eternal value unless the born-again person continues to walk by faith and live after the new nature of the Spirit, allowing God to complete the process that began at the new birth.

Holiness is not an option: it is a command that we are to implement in all aspects of our lives. "But as He who called you is holy, you also be holy in all your conduct, because it is written, 'Be holy, for I am holy'" (I Peter 1:15-16, NKJV).

2. Definition of Holiness

God is holy; holiness is an essential aspect of His nature. With respect to Him, it means absolute purity and moral perfection. With respect to humans, holiness means conformity to the character and will of God. It means thinking as God thinks, loving what He loves, hating what He hates, and acting as Christ would act. It means having the mind of Christ (I Corinthians 2:16; Philippians 2:5).

The Old Testament concept of holiness was "separation from and dedication to."[1] For example, the Sabbath was holy because it was separated from work, travel, and other mundane activities, and dedicated to rest. The Tabernacle vessels were holy because they were separated from all ordinary use and dedicated solely to sacred use.

God commanded His people to be holy (Leviticus 11:44; 19:2; 20:7)—separated from all other peoples and dedicated to the worship of the one true God. The Levitical laws separated the Israelites from all other nations in diet, clothing, appearance, farming practices, Sabbath observance, sanitation, and morality. These laws taught a clear distinction between the clean and unclean, the holy and profane (Leviticus 11:47; Ezekiel 22:26). The doctrine of holiness made Old Testament Judaism unique among ancient religious, particularly in its concept of separation and in its linkage of morality with religion.

The ceremonial law foreshadowed greater spiritual truths, teaching spiritual principles by physical types (Galatians 3:24-25; Hebrews 10:1). The new covenant abolished ceremonial types, while retaining moral law and spiritual holiness (Colossians 2:16-17).

Building on the Old Testament concept of holiness, the New Testament teaches a corresponding twofold definition of moral holiness for God's people: (1) *separation* from sin and the world system and (2) *dedication* to God and His will. Just as a person forsakes all other romantic relationships, actual or potential, to enjoy the total commitment of a marriage relationship, so we renounce worldly living as part of our new life in Christ.

"I beseech you therefore, brethren, by the mercies of God, that ye present your bodies a living sacrifice, holy, acceptable unto God, which is your reasonable service. And be not conformed to this world, but be ye transformed by the renewing of your mind" (Romans 12:1-2). "Wherefore come out from among them and be ye separate, saith the Lord, and touch not the unclean thing; and I will receive you. . . . Having therefore these promises, dearly beloved, let us cleanse ourselves from all filthiness of the flesh and spirit, perfecting holiness in the fear of God" (II Corinthians 6:17; 7:1). "Put off, concerning your former conduct, the old man which grows corrupt according to the deceitful lusts, and be renewed in the spirit of your mind, and . . . put on the new man which was created according to God, in righteousness and true holiness" (Ephesians 4:22-24, NKJV).

In sum, holiness means to imitate Christ, to be Christlike. The holy person will not gratify the desires of the sinful nature, but he will put on the personality and mind of Christ and will let Christ be formed in him (Romans 13:14; Galatians 4:19). He will judge every decision and every action by the question, What would Jesus do? All his words and deeds will be compatible with invoking the name of Jesus (Colossians 3:17). In everything he says and does he will be able to ask for Christ's assistance and presence.

3. Principles of Holiness

Holiness means that we are not to love this ungodly world system, identify with it, become attached to the things in it, or participate in its sinful pleasures and activities. "Know ye not that the friendship of the world is enmity with God? whosoever therefore will be a friend of the world is the enemy of God" (James 4:4). One important aspect of pure and undefiled religion is to keep "unspotted from the world" (James 1:27).

We specifically need to avoid three major areas of temptation and sin: lust of the flesh, lust of the eyes, and pride. "Love not the world, neither the things that are in the world. If any man love the world, the love of the

Father is not in him. For all that is in the world, the lust of the flesh, and the lust of the eyes, and the pride of life, is not of the Father, but is of the world" (I John 2:15-16). The purpose of holiness standards is to protect us in one or more of these areas.

Temperance is an important principle to implement in every aspect of daily living (I Corinthians 9:24-27). It means self-discipline, self-control, and moderation in all things. We are to deny self-will and surrender to the will of God.

As Christians we must abstain from all appearance of evil (I Thessalonians 5:22). We must flee from evil in whatever guise it appears and refuse to participate in anything that would associate us with evil in the eyes of others. If an activity is doubtful for us, we should avoid it (Romans 14:23).

Holiness involves both the inner person and the outer person (I Corinthians 6:19-20; I Thessalonians 5:23). We are to perfect holiness in our lives by cleansing ourselves of filthiness both of the spirit and of the flesh (II Corinthians 7:1). For example, lustful thoughts as well as acts of adultery are sinful (Matthew 5:27-28), and hatred as well as murder is sinful (I John 3:15).

Holiness, then, includes attitudes, thoughts, and spiritual stewardship on the one hand, and actions, appearance, and physical stewardship on the other. Both are necessary. With time and teaching a person who has a true spirit of holiness will manifest holiness outwardly, but the outward appearance of holiness is of little value without inward holiness. For example, a modest spirit will produce modest dress, but modest dress is of little value if it conceals a lustful heart.

The life of holiness is a continual striving for perfection (Matthew 5:48; II Corinthians 7:1; Philippians

3:12-16). No one is absolutely perfect, but each of us can be relatively perfect, or mature. We are holy if we place our faith in Christ, live a repented life according to God's Word, and seek to grow progressively more Christ-like by the power of the indwelling Spirit (Ephesians 4:13). God expects continual growth in grace and knowledge and increasing production of spiritual fruit (John 15:1-8; II Peter 3:18).

Holiness is a daily walk with the daily goal of overcoming sin (John 5:14; 8:11). As Christians we are not to sin; if we do, we can receive forgiveness by repentance and confession (I John 1:9; 2:1).

God evaluates each person on the basis of where he has come from, what God has given him, and what his potential is (Matthew 13:23; 25:14-30). Two Christians can both be perfect in God's sight even though they have attained different levels of perfection in an absolute sense, just as two children at two different stages of growth can both be perfectly normal and healthy.

We should not judge one another's motives or standing before God, nor should we compare one person with another (Matthew 7:1-5; II Corinthians 10:12). Instead, we must be patient and tolerant of different levels of perfection, endeavoring to maintain the unity of the Spirit in the bond of peace (Ephesians 4:1-3). In particular, we should take care not to condemn, intimidate, or offend anyone, especially visitors and new converts. At the same time, we must be faithful to biblical teaching and godly convictions without compromising or abandoning the position we have attained (Philippians 3:15-16).

4. The Purpose for Holiness

The first reason for holiness is *to please God*. We belong to God in a double sense: by creation and by redemption. Therefore, we have no right to live contrary to God's will. "What? know ye not that your body is the temple of the Holy Ghost which is in you, which you have of God, and ye are not your own? For ye are bought with a price: therefore glorify God in your body, and in your spirit, which are God's" (I Corinthians 6:19-20). "He died for all, that they which live should not henceforth live unto themselves, but unto him which died for them, and rose again" (II Corinthians 5:15). (See also I Peter 1:18-19.)

God created us for His glory (Isaiah 43:7), and He intended for us to love, worship, and commune with Him. Sin separated us from the holy God, however. Through the Cross, God provided a means of redemption and reconciliation so that we can be restored to fellowship with Him. If we persist in living in sin, however, we continue to separate ourselves from His presence. Only by living in holiness do we fulfill His purpose in both creation and redemption. "But you are a chosen generation, a royal priesthood, a holy nation, His own special people, that you may proclaim the praises of Him who called you out of darkness into His marvelous light" (I Peter 2:9, NKJV).

The second reason for holiness is *to communicate Christ to others.* People will be attracted to Christ only to the extent that they see Christ in us. They will believe our proclamation that Jesus saves from sin only if they can see the saving power of the gospel operative in our lives. People who are dissatisfied with their worldly life and who seek salvation will only be attracted to a church that is clearly different from the world.

A holy church will be able to lead sinners to the worship of God. "Let your light so shine before men, that they may see your good works, and glorify your Father which is in heaven" (Matthew 5:16). "Abstain from fleshly lusts which war against the soul, having your conduct

15

honorable among the Gentiles, that when they speak against you as evildoers, they may, by your good works which they observe, glorify God in the day of visitation" (I Peter 2:11-12, NKJV). We are epistles of Christ written by the Spirit, known and read by everyone (II Corinthians 3:2-3).

The third reason for holiness is *to benefit ourselves, both now and for eternity.* From the spiritual point of view, living for God is the logical, reasonable, and expected thing to do (Romans 12:1). The life of holiness brings great benefits in this life—physically, mentally, and spiritually—and it leads to eternal life. God designed humans to live according to holiness principles, and when those principles are violated great harm results. For example, such things as intemperance, sexual immorality, rage, and bitterness can actually cause physical illness. Those who live godly lives enjoy divine love, peace, joy, and hope. They truly have abundant life, now and for eternity.

5. Holiness As God's Nature

The call to holiness is rooted in the very nature of God. We are to be holy in everything we do because the God we serve is holy (I Peter 1:15-16). Those who reject moral law and practical holiness fail to understand that holiness is the fundamental characteristic of God upon which all His other moral attributes depend. In particular, God's holiness is the foundation of His love and gives direction to His love. His holiness determines His love, not vice versa. Because He is holy, He does not love sin or evil. Because He is holy, His love is impartial and eternal rather than arbitrary, capricious, or fickle. God's love does not contradict or override His holiness.

Sin is a direct challenge to God's sovereignty and a violation of His holiness. God's love will never cause Him to overlook sin, because sin contradicts His basic nature of holiness. When God forgives sin He does not simply excuse it, but He accepts Christ's death as the sufficient penalty for that sin. In this way, God's love provides forgiveness without violating His justice. "God presented him as a sacrifice of atonement, through faith in his blood. He did this to demonstrate his justice, because in his forbearance he had left the sins committed beforehand unpunished" (Romans 3:25, NIV). The Cross shows that God demands punishment for all sin. If we place our faith in Christ (which includes repentance from sin and obedience to Him), then we apply Christ's death to our lives to cleanse us from sin. Otherwise, we will receive punishment for our sin.

6. The Source of Holiness Teaching
The supreme source of holiness teaching is the Bible itself, which is the inspired Word of God. It contains everything we need to know concerning salvation and godly living. "The holy scriptures . . . are able to make thee wise unto salvation through faith which is in Christ Jesus. All scripture is given by inspiration of God, and is profitable for doctrine, for reproof, for correction, for instruction in righteousness: that the man of God may be perfect, throughly furnished unto all good works" (II Timothy 3:15-17).

All holiness teaching must come from the Bible. A true holiness standard is either (1) a specific biblical statement or (2) a valid application of a biblical principle. For example, the Bible specifically teaches that drunkenness is sinful, so we must acknowledge and teach that truth. In addition, the underlying biblical principle is that all intoxication is wrong; therefore we should abstain from intoxicating drugs such as marijuana and cocaine, even though the Bible does not mention them by name.

The Bible is not merely a collection of rules. It does not try to give specific answers to the countless situations that may face an individual. Rather, it contains basic guidelines that apply to people of all cultures, times, and situations.

To help His people understand and live by scriptural principles, God has given the church spiritual leaders. Their task is to equip the saints for the building up, maturing, establishing, and growth of the body (Ephesians 4:11-16). Spirit-filled pastors and teachers proclaim God's Word, explain it, and apply its principles to the situations of contemporary life.

Finally, the Holy Spirit teaches us directly through internal promptings and convictions. The Spirit is given to teach and guide us (John 14:26; 16:13). The Spirit writes God's laws upon our hearts (Jeremiah 31:33). We have an anointing—a fundamental nature of holiness and truth that resides within—that no one has taught us (I John 2:27). In times of decision, struggle, crisis, or uncertainty, we should be sensitive to the still, quiet voice of the Spirit.

The three holiness teachers—*(1) the Bible, (2) spiritual leadership, and (3) the indwelling Holy Spirit*—work together in harmony and complement one another. The Bible is our final authority. God does not give human beings the right to change His message, nor will the indwelling Spirit speak contrary to the written Word He Himself inspired.

7. The Motivation for Holiness

Holiness is not a means of earning salvation but a result of salvation. As such, it comes by grace through faith (Ephesians 2:8-9). Holiness does not come by works of the flesh but only by submission to the Holy Spirit's leadership. We cannot manufacture our own holiness; we can only be partakers of God's holiness (Hebrews 12:10).

Holiness is both instantaneous and progressive. As Christians we received immediate sanctification (separation from sin) when we repented, were baptized in Jesus' name, and received the Holy Spirit (I Corinthians 6:11). God counted us as holy by imputing the righteousness of Christ to us. Even so, we must follow after holiness (Hebrews 12:14). We are already sanctified, but we are also called to be saints (sanctified, holy ones) (I Corinthians 1:2).

Holiness comes by *(1) faith, (2) love, and (3) walking after the Spirit,* which provide the basis, foundation, motivation, and power for holiness.

First, genuine faith in God inevitably results in obedience to God (Acts 6:7; Romans 1:5; 10:16; 16:26; James 2:14-26). If we believe God we will believe His Word, and if we believe His Word we will accept its teachings and apply them to our lives. By faith we accept Christ's atonement as sufficient for our salvation and apply His death, burial, and resurrection to our lives. Specifically, by faith we die to sin in repentance, are buried with Jesus Christ in baptism for the remission of sins, and receive new life through the Holy Spirit, who enables us to live holy. By faith we continue to walk with God until the ultimate work of salvation—glorification.

Along with faith in God, we need a love for God, His Word, and holiness. Without love, all attempts to live for God are vain (I Corinthians 13:1-13; Revelation 2:1-7). If we love God, we will obey His commandments and seek to implement holiness in our lives (John 14:15, 23; I John 2:3-6). When we truly love God, we will actively hate evil (Psalm 97:10) and we will seek to become like our holy

God. The greater our love for God, the greater our desire for holiness.

Love is far stricter and more demanding than law, for love always goes farther than duty. Love for God will cause someone to draw much closer to God than legalism will, both in attitudes and in disciplined living. Love will cause someone to avoid everything that displeases God or that hinders a closer walk with God. Love rejects everything that is not clearly compatible with godliness, or that is not conducive to Christianity, even though no rules have specifically labelled these things as sin. In this way, the principle of love leads to greater holiness than does the law of Moses or a codification of rules.

Love dominates all actions and all relationships. All the law is summed up in love: we are to love God with all our being and to love our fellow humans as we love ourselves (Matthew 22:36-40; Romans 13:9-10). Instead of the law of Moses we have "the perfect law of liberty," which is the "royal law" of love (James 1:25; 2:8; 2:12).

Since holiness is God's very nature, when we receive the Holy Spirit of God we receive a holy nature. Through the Spirit's power, we can overcome sin and live righteously (Romans 8:2-4; Galatians 5:16; I Thessalonians 4:7-8). We have freedom from sin's dominion—the power to choose not to sin (John 8:34-36; Romans 6:1-25). We will not continue to live in sin, and in fact our newly given nature cannot sin (I John 3:9). We still have the ability to sin and we still have the sinful nature subdued within us (Galatians 5:16-17; I John 1:8; 2:1), but the born-again nature restrains us from habitually committing sin. As long as we let the Spirit lead us we will not sin.

Holiness is not an external law but an integral part of the new nature. The Spirit places God's moral law within us, not written on tables of stone but written in our hearts

(Jeremiah 31:33; Hebrews 10:16). In living for God, we do not merely follow an outward list of rules, but we follow the nature of the Holy Spirit within us. We live holy because that is what the new man is and wants to be. We abstain from sin and worldliness because it is anathema to our new nature. We still struggle against the continual desires and lusts of the old nature, but it is an internal struggle. No dictator imposes rules on us; we impose restrictions on the sinful nature because we no longer wish to follow the flesh but to follow the Spirit.

One author commented on Romans 8:2-4, "Christian holiness is not a matter of painstaking conformity to the individual precepts of an external law-code; it is rather a question of the Holy Spirit's producing His fruit in the life, reproducing those graces which were seen in perfection in the life of Christ. The law prescribed a life of holiness, but it was powerless to produce such a life, because of the inadequacy of the human material that it had to work upon. But what the law was powerless to do has been done by God. . . . All that the law required by way of conformity to the will of God is now realized in the lives of those who are controlled by the Holy Spirit and are released from their servitude to the old order. God's commands have now become God's enablings."[2]

Following holiness requires personal effort; it is not automatic. Some teach that any attempt to live holy is "of the flesh," but genuine faith always includes obedience and always produces good works. We must open our lives to the working of God's Spirit and actively implement spiritual principles. The Bible commands us to reckon ourselves dead to sin but alive to God, yield our bodily members to God instead of sin, resist the devil, draw near to God, subdue the sinful nature, discipline the flesh, kill the deeds of the body, cleanse ourselves, labor to enter into rest, lay aside every weight and sin, and run with patience. "Make every effort to be found spotless, blameless, and at peace with him" (II Peter 3:14, NIV).

Philippians 2:12-13 charges us, "Work out your own salvation with fear and trembling. For it is God which worketh in you both to will and to do of his good pleasure." God actually performs the work of salvation, providing the desire and the power to live righteously, but we must reverently and watchfully implement holiness in our lives.

One writer explained, "The pursuit of holiness is a joint venture between God and the Christian. No one can attain any degree of holiness without God working in his life, but just as surely no one will attain it without effort on his own part. God has made it possible for us to walk in holiness. But He has given to us the responsibility of doing the walking; He does not do that for us. . . . We pray for victory when we know we should be acting in obedience."[3]

As an analogy, a farmer is totally dependent upon God for sunshine, rain, and the miracle of life in the seed. Nevertheless, he will not have a crop unless he cultivates, plants, tends, and harvests. In short, we cannot do what God must do, but God will not do what we can do.

8. Legalism

Legalism means strict or excessive conformity to a legal code or set of rules. In a Christian context, legalism has two negative connotations: (1) basing salvation on good works or on strict observance of law and (2) imposing nonbiblical rules. The Bible strongly condemns legalism in this sense (Matthew 23; Romans 3-4; Galatians 3).

Law is helpful as a line of demarcation, a minimum standard, or a safety net, but ultimately it is insufficient to produce holiness. As we have already seen, true holiness comes by faith, love, and the Spirit. They are the proper alternatives to legalism, and they will actually lead to far more self-discipline than law can.

For example, law, or fear of getting caught, can cause a man to remain physically faithful to his wife and restrain him in a time of temptation, but he may still be very unfaithful in thoughts, attitudes, behavior, and flirtations. By contrast, true love for his wife will drive away all contrary thoughts and desires, and in the long run only love will make the marriage a true success. Similarly, a person who seeks to serve God merely by rules will ultimately fail, because he will face situations that his rules do not specifically address and because he will lack the inward principles and convictions needed to guide him.

Sometimes leaders present biblical standards of holiness as a set of rules and regulations, justifying them only by tradition and human authority. In rebelling against this legalistic approach, some people discard true holiness principles and valid practical applications. The problem on both sides is a failure to commit quality time in serious, prayerful study of the Word of God.

Many wrongly suppose that the proper alternative to legalism is antinomianism (no law), license (freedom without responsibility), or libertinism (no moral restraints). True holiness is not "freedom" to act and look like the world, however, but freedom from the need to conform to the world. Genuine spiritual freedom is not "freedom" to commit sin, but freedom from sin's bondage.

There can be no real freedom outside truth (John 8:32). Spiritual freedom is not freedom from truth, but freedom to know and submit to the truth. For example, a man who is ignorant of the law of gravity and therefore walks off a cliff unconcernedly is not free. Rather, he is free when he understands the danger of walking off the cliff and has the ability to avoid doing so, thereby preserving his life and liberty. A Christian is free because he knows what sin is and how deadly it is and has the power to overcome it.

As Christians we still have commandments to obey (Matthew 28:20; John 14:15, 23). The ceremonial law has been abolished, but we still must not participate in spiritually unclean things (II Corinthians 6:17). The Christian life is like a contest, with spiritual guidelines that we must follow. "And also if anyone competes in athletics, he is not crowned unless he competes according to the rules" (II Timothy 2:5, NKJV).

Moral law is a restraining force, but the sinful nature needs a restraint upon its desires, while the spiritual man needs protection against evil. Like a fence around a garden, holiness teachings do not curb our freedom in Christ but preserve it. Like gravity keeping the earth in orbit around the sun, they bind us closely to our holy God, who is our source of life and strength. Like train tracks or the banks of a river, they keep us on course, preserve our identity, and channel our spiritual energy.

9. Christian Liberty

Biblical Christianity is not a life of bondage but a life of liberty. This liberty does not eliminate the call to holiness, however. We can identify three aspects of Christian liberty.

1. *Freedom from sin.* Sin and God's will are mutually exclusive, so by definition, to be free from one means to submit to the other. To exercise Christian liberty means to break free from sin's bondage, which means to obey and serve God, which in turn means to serve "right-

eousness unto holiness" and to bear "fruit unto holiness" (Romans 6:15-23).

2. *Freedom from the law.* God has not abolished moral law, but Christians are free from Old Testament law in several ways:

*Freedom from the penalty of the law—death. Christ died in our stead, so the law has no power to condemn us.

*Freedom from the attempt to fulfill the law by human effort alone. Old Testament saints were bound to the law like children under tutors and governors (Galatians 4). They could not fully overcome the flesh and keep God's moral law, but the Spirit now gives us power to do so (Romans 8:2-4).

*Freedom from the destructive power of the law caused by abuse of it. The law, which was good in itself, actually became a harmful force because people erroneously relied on it for justification and so rejected faith in Christ (Romans 9:31-10:3).

*Freedom from the ceremonial law (Mark 7:15; Acts 15; Galatians 4; Colossians 2:16-17).

3. *Freedom in nonmoral matters.* We can participate in any activity that does not violate biblical teaching. We have freedom to follow individual judgment, desire, and conscience in morally neutral areas such as eating of meat and observance of certain days (Romans 14). In these matters, we are not to judge each other, but we are to be true to our own convictions.

Christian liberty does not negate the responsibility to obey scriptural holiness teachings (Romans 6:15; Galatians 5:13). Nor does it eliminate the responsibility to follow godly leaders when they apply biblical principles of holiness to contemporary issues (Acts 15:28-29; Hebrews 13:17).

The Bible gives four guidelines for the proper exercise of Christian liberty in nonmoral matters.[4] Namely, we should:

1. *Do everything to the glory of God* (I Corinthians 10:31; Colossians 3:17).

2. *Avoid anything that is not beneficial to us* (I Corinthians 6:12; 10:23). We should abstain from things detrimental to us physically, mentally, or spiritually. We should lay aside every "weight," or hindrance, as well as outright sin (Hebrews 12:1).

3. *Avoid anything that would gain dominance over us* (I Corinthians 6:12). We must not let anything addict us, rob us of too much energy, time or money, or interfere with our relationship to God.

4. *Avoid anything that would harm others* (Romans 14:13-21; I Corinthians 8:9-13; 10:32-33). We should avoid things that could cause someone else to stumble.

If the Bible condemns a practice either specifically or in principle, obedience is necessary. If the four basic guidelines for the proper exercise of Christian liberty point to a certain course of action, then again obedience is necessary. For example, eating meat offered to idols fell under the scope of Christian liberty, yet the apostolic church absolutely forbade the practice because it was a stumbling block. If an issue is morally neutral and the four guidelines do not define a certain response, then the teachings of Romans 14 apply.

10. The Practical Application of Holiness

It is possible to classify holiness standards in two categories.

1. *Clear teachings of Scripture.* Examples are the teachings against fornication, lying, and drunkenness. Bible believers should agree on these standards, and the

new convert should begin to follow them immediately. A pastor should refuse to baptize someone who does not manifest a desire and willingness to obey these biblical injunctions.

2. *Practical applications of scriptural principles to modern situations.* Examples are practices related to adornment, dress, and amusements. New converts usually understand and implement these teachings gradually as they grow in grace and knowledge. Christians can have legitimate differences of opinion, not on principles, but on a precise application in a specific situation. For the sake of unity and a clear witness to the community, however, they should follow the teachings of their pastor in these matters, for God has entrusted him with the oversight and care of the local church.

New converts may not conform immediately, especially if they lack a strong biblical background. The pastor should lead them patiently into further truth, relying on scriptural teaching, Christian example, and the work of the Spirit. God has justified them by their faith, but they must submit to the progressive work of sanctification. The pastor should not use them to lead or represent the local church until they implement these teachings.

Here are important areas in which biblical, and therefore universal and unchanging, principles of holiness apply.[5]

1. *Attitudes* (Galatians 5:19-23; Ephesians 4:23-32). We must put away evil attitudes such as hatred, wrath, envy, jealousy, covetousness (greed), bitterness, malice, pride, prejudice, vengeance, and all discord (contention, strife, selfish ambition, dissension, clamor, brawling, murmuring, complaining, rebellion, a critical spirit). The essence of holiness is bearing the fruit of the Spirit—love, joy, peace, longsuffering (patience), gentleness (kindness),

goodness, faith (faithfulness), meekness (gentleness), and temperance (self-control). We must learn to forgive, to be obedient to authority, to be thankful, not to let anything offend us, and not to be busybodies in others' lives.

2. *Thoughts* (Matthew 5:18-20; II Corinthians 10:5; Philippians 4:8). A person is what he thinks, and he becomes what he allows his mind to dwell upon. We are to think on true, honest (noble), just (right), pure, lovely, reputable, virtuous (excellent), and praiseworthy things. We must cast out evil thoughts, taking captive every thought to make it obedient to Christ. Temptation is not sin, but entertaining and retaining evil thoughts is.

3. *The tongue* (James 1:26; 3:1-12; 4:1; 5:12). We must avoid talebearing, backbiting, slander, sowing discord, swearing by oath, using the Lord's name in vain, pronouncement of curses, reviling, lying, idle words, and suggestive, indecent, or obscene speech.

4. *The eye* (Psalm 101:3; 119:37; Matthew 6:22-23). The eye is the gate of the soul and the primary source of input for the mind. We should not read materials saturated with vulgarity and sensuality. Because violence, illicit sex, lust, evil speech, sinfulness, and vanity dominate television and movies, we should not own a television or watch movies (at the theater or on video). These media subtly undermine spiritual values and priorities and feed carnal desires.

5. *Appearance (adornment, dress, and hair)* (Deuteronomy 22:5; I Corinthians 11:1-16; I Timothy 2:8-10; I Peter 3:1-5). The appearance reflects the inner self, both to God and to others. A worldly appearance promotes lust of the flesh, lust of the eyes, pride of life, artificiality, and false values, molding both wearer and society in ungodly ways.

Important biblical principles in this area are (1)

modesty, (2) rejection of ornamentation, (3) moderation in cost, (4) distinction between male and female, and (5) separation from worldliness. Thus we should abstain from clothing that immodestly exposes the body; ornamental jewelry; colored cosmetics and hair dye; very expensive, extravagant, or gaudy attire; dresses or skirts on men; pants on women; long hair on men; cut hair on women; and fashions with carnal associations.

It is vitally important to teach principles, not just rules, to avoid inconsistencies in this area. Men must be careful to avoid effeminate styles, and women masculine styles. Since God asks women to have long hair, they should not trim it or otherwise seek to shorten it deliberately. It is inconsistent to object to lipstick but wear blush or mascara. It is likewise inconsistent to object to earrings or nose rings but wear finger rings for ornamentation.

It violates scriptural principles to be extremely costly, extravagant, showy, or ostentatious in hairstyle, clothing, or functional jewelry (jewelry worn for function, not ornament, such as a watch). Four questions will help determine when these things are too extravagant: (1) What is the motive for wearing it? (2) Is it wise stewardship? (3) How do others view it? (4) What would Jesus do?

6. *Stewardship of the body* (I Corinthians 3:16-17; 6:12, 19-20). The body is the temple of the Spirit, so we should not use things that harm or defile the body, cause intoxication, or cause addiction. Alcoholic beverages, tobacco, and illegal drugs violate this principle. Other problems in this area are gluttony, obesity due to overindulgence, abuse of legal drugs, and caffeine addiction.

7. *Sanctity of marriage* (I Corinthians 6:9-10; Colossians 3:5; Hebrews 13:4). The Bible condemns all sexual relations outside the permanent marriage of a man and a woman. It opposes lustful thoughts and

actions. Youth must flee from fornication and lustful caressing when dating. Since God's plan is lifelong marriage, we should not follow worldly examples and seek divorce on grounds of mistake, incompatibility, or falling out of love.

8. *Sanctity of human life* (Exodus 20:13; Matthew 5:39, 44). We should not condone violence, and we should personally reject all intentional killing of human beings, even in abortion, warfare, and suicide.

9. *Honesty and integrity* (Mark 10:19). The Bible rejects all forms of dishonesty and corruption, including lying, stealing, defrauding, refusal to pay debts, extortion, bribery, and cheating.

10. *Fellowship* (Matthew 18:15-18; I Corinthians 5:9-6:8; 15:33; II Corinthians 6:14). We must not become identified with sinful attitudes or lifestyles. We should not have fellowship with so-called Christians who continually indulge in sinful activities, nor become yoked with unbelievers (such as by marriage). In the church, we are to resolve all disputes according to the procedure given by Christ, not by suing one another in civil court.

11. *Worldly activities* (I Thessalonians 5:22; Titus 3:3; I John 2:15). We must maturely regulate music, sports, games, and amusements. To the extent possible, we should avoid places or events with atmospheres, influences, or associations that are excessively worldly. For example, many otherwise acceptable activities and entertainments take place in an atmosphere filled with immodesty, lewdness, cursing, drinking, extreme rivalry, and violence, and Christians are not at home in such surroundings. Some amusements are inherently worldly, such as gambling, dancing, hard rock music, astrology, and occult practices.

11. Holiness and Culture

These holiness principles have received much endorsement historically. Most or all have been taught by ante-Nicene church fathers of the second and third centuries, various medieval groups, Anabaptists, early Calvinists, Puritans, Pietists, early Methodists, Holiness churches, and Pentecostals.[6] Changing culture has caused most of the spiritual heirs of these groups to abandon many of these teachings. But how much should culture affect holiness standards? Several truths must be noted in answering this question.

1. *God's moral law is unchanging.* God's nature does not change, so moral laws based on God's holiness remain invariant in all times, places, cultures, and circumstances. God has abolished Old Testament types and ceremonial laws—such as dietary laws, blood sacrifices, sabbaths, and feasts—but He has never abrogated moral law.

2. *Biblical principles are unchanging.* The Bible is the inspired, infallible, authoritative Word of God. It is truth, and truth is absolute, immutable, and constant.

3. *God has progressively revealed truth from Old to New Testament.* The New Testament does not contradict Old Testament truth but unfolds God's will more completely and calls Spirit-filled believers to a higher level of perfection in many areas. In such cases, the Old Testament usually contains indications of God's higher plan. Examples are incest, polygamy, divorce, warfare, adornment, and use of alcohol.

4. *God gave His Word in a specific cultural setting, but He did not thereby endorse all the practices of that culture.* Christians are not bound to follow the culture of biblical times unless it expresses eternal truths endorsed by the Bible. For example, the Bible describes but does not require arranged marriages. Some aspects

of culture in biblical times were actually unchristian, but the Bible gave instructions for believers to cope with them. Examples are oppressive government and slavery.

5. *In applying a biblical principle to a modern situation, we must take culture into account, but culture never abolishes the principle.* For example, to some degree modesty is culturally relative. In the nineteenth century it was improper for a woman to expose any of her leg in public, so Christian women of that day should not have worn knee-length dresses. For the biblical teaching on modesty to have meaning, however, there must be a minimum absolute of modesty. Otherwise, if society condoned total nudity, so could Christians.

How can we determine what is culturally relative and what is not? First, the biblical principle involved will point to a minimum standard regardless of culture. Second, the Bible often makes specific applications. If the Bible speaks of something approvingly or neutrally then it is not wrong under all circumstances. If the Bible always speaks disapprovingly of something, then apparently it always violates biblical principles.

For example, what principles are involved in modesty of dress? Immodest dress promotes lust of the flesh, lust of the eyes, and pride of life. The exposed body tends to arouse improper thoughts in both wearer and onlooker. This indicates that clothes should basically cover the body—the torso and upper limbs. Moreover, according to Isaiah 47:2-3, God considers baring the leg and uncovering the thigh to be shameful exposure and nakedness.

The Bible speaks of beards favorably or neutrally, and they are a natural part of the male appearance. They are not inherently evil but are wrong only if associated with a sinful lifestyle, rebellion, or pride. During the hippie era they generally did have worldly connotations of this kind, but as culture removes those associations, we need not object to them.

Culture determines the distinction between male and female dress. For example, the kilt in traditional Scotland was exclusively masculine so it did not violate the principle of separation between male and female. Women's pants today, violate this principle, however, even though some are designed exclusively for women. They still "pertain to a man," contrary to Deuteronomy 22:5. They are patterned after the masculine dress style, they promote masculine behavior patterns, they do not distinguish gender clearly in the overall appearance (by silhouette or at a distance), and they leave males without a distinctive dress style. Often they are immodest as well.

Modern culture accepts makeup, no longer connecting it with harlotry. The Bible always links makeup with evil, however (Jeremiah 4:30; Ezekiel 23:40). Moreover, makeup still promotes lust of the flesh, lust of the eyes, pride of life, artificiality, discontent with God's creative work, and false values. It still contradicts the biblical teaching to be modest and shamefaced and to reject ornamentation.

Modern culture promotes the cutting of women's hair, but the Bible always links this practice with shame and unnaturalness. Moreover, I Corinthians 11:5-6 and 13-16 explicitly teach that God desires for all women, regardless of culture, to have long hair.

12. Areas of Concern

In light of the biblical teachings on holiness, the church should respond in a positive manner to overcome inconsistencies or weaknesses that may emerge. Here are some areas that warrant attention.

*Commitment to God's Word. When Christians fail to

study Bible doctrine in a disciplined, systematic way, they often discard holiness under influence from friends, relatives, and various religious groups. Without the support of God's Word, preachers cannot stand against opposition, persecution, and adversity; but they will compromise truth for social and religious acceptance, material gain, numerical growth, or worldly success.

*Practical holiness teaching. Christians need to hear teaching on specific subjects such as the fruit of the Spirit, attitudes, sins of the tongue, and lust of the eyes. Holiness issues are important to address not only during times of obvious failures but on a regular basis.

*Teaching outward holiness. It is wrong to assume that if we are sincere or if our motives are right then it does not really matter what we wear, where we go, what we do, or what we watch. Carelessness in these areas can lead to carnality and sin.

*Teaching inward holiness. It is wrong to equate holiness with dress codes instead of the fruit of the Spirit and Christ-like attitudes. The outward appearance of holiness cannot cover sins of the spirit; holiness of spirit is essential.

*Avoiding legalism. The essence of holiness is a positive transformation of character, not a list of negative rules. It is important to realize that we cannot base salvation on works of holiness. When preachers enforce rules by their own authority without providing biblical support, they promote a form of legalism. Legalism often leads to undeveloped inward holiness, misunderstanding of biblical principles, misapplication of those principles, living by minimum requirements, looking for legal loopholes, hypocrisy, inconsistency, disillusionment, rebellion, and condemnatory attitudes.

*Avoiding a judgmental, condemnatory attitude. Peo-

34

ple with this attitude often wound and drive away visitors, new converts, and even longtime believers.

*Emphasizing godly living as well as emotional experiences. Spiritual gifts and worship expressions (such as speaking in tongues and dancing in the Spirit) demonstrate God's gracious blessings and a person's surrender to these manifestations, but the fruit of the Spirit is the evidence of the Spirit's continuing leadership and control. A life of obedient faith and holiness is the expression of true spirituality.

There are professional or social churchgoers who enjoy Christian fellowship, music, worship, and preaching but who are not committed to true holiness. Sometimes their family connections, social status, or talents cause them to be promoted despite their lack of dedication.

*Overcoming greed and materialism (I Timothy 6:7-19). Some people greedily accumulate luxuries and material wealth at the expense of spiritual priorities. When preachers make spiritual decisions primarily on financial considerations, they discredit their call as ministers of the gospel. If they are drawn toward the ministry because it appears financially attractive, their service will be governed by materialism. God's people are not to follow the "gospel" of material prosperity, but they are to live modestly and give sacrificially of their time and finances.

*Overcoming prejudice and favoritism. God shows no partiality; He does not regard gender, social class, or race (Acts 10:34; Galatians 3:28). Christian leaders are not to show favoritism (I Timothy 5:21). Racial or social prejudice is sinful (James 2:9). Churches must not ignore or reject minority groups, nor should they condone racial hatred. Nepotism, cronyism, and other forms of favoritism have no place in the church.

*Overcoming pride. Christians must not succumb to a spirit of competition and accumulate status symbols. When preachers follow egotistical patterns of the world and build personal kingdoms, they cause contention and confusion.

*Conduct between male and female. The trend of the world is to engage in indiscriminate touching, embracing, and bold talk between male and female. When someone crosses these bounds of propriety and intimacy, however, seemingly innocent situations can give rise to temptation and sin.

Conclusion

The key to maintaining scriptural holiness is to promote a genuine love for God's Word. We must stress the authority of Scripture, the principles of holiness, the positive nature of holiness, Christian attitudes, holiness of spirit, spiritual fruit, and biblical reasons for holiness standards. We must teach and implement practical holiness, consciously seeking to develop and maintain a biblical world view and a Christian lifestyle.

At the same time, we must avoid legalism and its dangers. We must adhere to God's Word, proclaiming neither more nor less. We must be flexible in areas of Christian liberty, not insisting on tradition or personal taste. We must not be harsh or intolerant but wise, patient, and loving in presenting holiness to others.

In conclusion, holiness covers the entire realm of Christian living. The basis of holiness is faith, love, and walking after the Spirit. The power to live holy is a gift from God, but we are responsible to implement holiness on a daily basis. We can certainly walk in holiness if we will teach, preach, study, believe, love, and obey God's Word.

Holiness is an integral part of the salvation of the whole person from the power and effects of sin. It is a joyful privilege, a part of abundant life, a blessing from God's grace, a glorious life of freedom and power. The life of holiness fulfills God's original intention and design for humanity. For the Holy Spirit–filled believer who truly loves God, holiness is the normal—indeed the only—way to live.

Notes

[1]Isidore Epstein, *Judaism* (Middlesex, England: Penguin Books, 1959), p. 23.

[2]F. F. Bruce, *The Epistle of Paul to the Romans*, vol. 6 of *The Tyndale New Testament Commentaries*, R. V. G. Tasker (ed.) (Grand Rapids: Eerdmans, 1963), pp. 153, 156.

[3]Jerry Bridges, *The Pursuit of Holiness* (Colorado Springs: NavPress, 1978), p. 14.

[4]See ibid., p. 91.

[5]For a detailed discussion of each of these topics, see Loretta Bernard and David Bernard, *In Search of Holiness* (Hazelwood, Mo.: Word Aflame Press, 1981); David Bernard, *Practical Holiness: A Second Look* (Hazelwood, Mo.: Word Aflame Press, 1985).

[6]For documentation, see Bernard, *Practical Holiness*, especially chapter 5.

Tip #1

How to fit 103 books in a briefcase

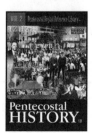

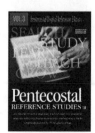

Solution:
The Pentecostal Digital Reference Library